What's the difference between . . .

Lenses and Prisms
and Other Scientific Things?

D1130021

Now available in Wiley's What's the Difference? Series:

What's the Difference Between Lenses and Prisms and Other Scientific Things?
    by Gary Soucie

What's the Difference Between Apes and Monkeys and Other Living Things?
    by Gary Soucie

What's the difference between . . .
Lenses and Prisms and Other Scientific Things?

Gary Soucie

Illustrated by Jeff Domm

John Wiley & Sons, Inc.
New York • Chichester • Brisbane • Toronto • Singapore

This one's for
Nick and Vladik

© 1995 by Gary A. Soucie
Illustrations © 1995 by Jeff Domm
Published by John Wiley & Sons, Inc.

Library of Congress Cataloging-in-Publication Data
Soucie, Gary.
    What's the difference between lenses and prisms and other scientific things? /
Gary Soucie: illustrated by Jeff Domm.
        Includes index.
        ISBN 0-471-08626-6 (alk. paper)
        1. Science—Miscellanea—Juvenile literature.   2. Technology—Miscellanea—
Juvenile literature.   3. Children's questions and answers.   [1. Science—
Miscellanea.   2. Technology—Miscellanea.   3. Questions and answers.
    I. Domm. Jeff. 1958–
    Q163.S715   1995
    500—dc20   95-10235
                                                                        AC

Printed in the United States of America

10 9 8 7 6 5 4 3 2 1

Contents

About This Book   **vii**

Science   1

What's the difference between
Theories and Hypotheses?   2

What's the difference between
Arithmetic and Mathematics?   4

What's the difference between
Cardinal and Ordinal Numbers?   6

What's the difference between
Analog and Digital?   8

What's the difference between
Fahrenheit and Celsius?   10

What's the difference between
Cycles and Phases?   12

What's the difference between
Mass and Weight?   14

What's the difference between
Tons and Tonnes?   16

What's the difference between
Liquids and Fluids?   18

What's the difference between
Elastic and Plastic?   20

What's the difference between
Concave and Convex?   22

What's the difference between
Lenses and Prisms?   24

What's the difference between
Radiation and Radioactivity?   26

What's the difference between
Wavelength, Frequency, and
Amplitude?   28

What's the difference between
Incandescent and Fluorescent?   30

What's the difference between
Sound and Noise?   32

What's the difference between
Oxygen and Ozone?   34

What's the difference between
Atoms and Molecules?   36

What's the difference between
Protons, Neutrons, and
Electrons?   38

What's the difference between
Fission and Fusion?   40

What's the difference between
Static Electricity and
Current Electricity?   42

Technology   45

What's the difference between
Minerals and Metals?   46

What's the difference between
Copper, Brass,and Bronze?   48

What's the difference between
Iron and Steel?   50

What's the difference between
Steel and Stainless Steel?   52

What's the difference between
Oil and Gasoline?   54

What's the difference between
Soaps and Detergents?   56

What's the difference between
Magnets and Electromagnets?   58

What's the difference between
Motors and Engines?   60

What's the difference between
Cranes and Derricks?   62

What's the difference between
Cement and Concrete?   64

What's the difference between
Microscopes and Electron
Microscopes?   66

What's the difference between
Telescopes and Radio Telescopes?   68

What's the difference between
Film and Videotape?   70

What's the difference between
Batteries and Dry Cells?   72

What's the difference between
Transformers and Transistors?   74

What's the difference between
Radar and Sonar?   76

What's the difference between
Bits and Bytes?   78

What's the difference between
RAM and ROM?   80

What's the difference between
CDs and CD-ROM Disks?   82

Glossary   84

Index   87

About This Book

This book looks at the differences between lots of things in the world of science and technology that many people tend to confuse. Sometimes the differences between things are small, and easily overlooked, but every distinction is important to scientists.

It may surprise you to learn that these distinctions are not always simple or neat. Scientists may know a lot about how things work or how to use them, and still not know for sure exactly what they are. That uncertainty is part of what makes science so fascinating.

How This Book Works

The book is divided into two sections. The first answers questions about the so-called "hard sciences"—chemistry and physics—plus a little mathematics. The second covers technology.

As an example of how each entry is set up, let's begin with this question:

What's the difference between . . .
Science and Technology?

Science is the study of things in nature and the universe, and the knowledge that this study produces. Technology is the use of scientific knowledge to serve society and people.

Science is based on searching for facts through careful observation and orderly experimentation. Sometimes, theories, laws, and other conclusions may be drawn from the scientific evidence. Science isn't in the facts themselves, but in the way the facts are determined and how the facts are used.

Technology is a marriage of knowledge and know-how. It applies the knowledge of science and the know-how of **engineering** to industrial processes. Science seeks to answer basic questions and technology tries to solve practical problems. Something called "applied science" falls sort of in between. It's the study of how to put science to practical use, how to *do* things.

During the eighteenth and early nineteenth centuries, many scientists—including Benjamin Franklin, Charles-Augustin de Coulomb, Alessandro Volta, André-Marie Ampère, and Michael Faraday—conducted important experiments that told them many things about electricity and how it works. That was science.

When Thomas Edison invented the first electric lightbulb in 1879, that was applied science. Soon thereafter, Edison, Nikola Tesla, and others developed ways to generate and distribute large amounts of electricity to lightbulbs, run motors, and do other useful **work**. That was technology.

Did you know?

- Sometimes technological gadgets were developed before the science behind them was known. Here's an example: Hero of Alexandria, who lived in Egypt during the first century B.C., took a metal sphere with two faucetlike vents attached and filled it with water. The sphere was then suspended over a fire between two brackets. When the water in the sphere boiled, steam escaped from the vents, causing the sphere to spin. It wasn't much of a scientific advancement, because Hero never developed a hypothesis or theory about what was happening. Nor could it be called a technological development, because no one knew what it was good for. So the world's first steam turbine and jet engine was just an amusing toy.

Okay, now you know how it works. You might have noticed that a few words in this book—such as **engineering** and **work** in our example—are printed in **boldface**. Just in case you don't know these words, they are defined in a glossary at the end of the book. Using this book is easier than going to a dictionary or encyclopedia, but you should refer to them often whenever you are wondering about science and technology.

You can read this book from cover to cover, dip into it at random, or look up specific things you want to know about. You can also use it as a game to play with family and friends. Just read the questions aloud and see whether anyone knows the answers. And don't forget the *Did you know?* questions.

If you want to keep score, award points for correct answers. A straightforward question that has a single answer could be worth one, five, ten, or however many points you want to use. If the answer is a list of things, you can award a single point for each correct response.

If you have a lot of people in the game, you might divide them into teams of two, three, or four and let them compete for points. You can ask questions of each player (or team) in turn, or you can throw the question out and let the player who first raises a hand, rings a bell, or shouts, "I know!" have the first shot at it. You've watched game shows on television. You know the different ways to do it.

However you decide to use this book, I hope you learn a lot of neat things and have a lot of fun. I did while writing it.

Science

What's the difference between . . . Theories and Hypotheses?

A hypothesis is the unproven, but logical, idea being tested in a scientific experiment or investigation. A theory is a general principle or set of principles that explains specific facts or events of the natural world.

A theory is assumed to be true because it is based on other phenomena that are proven or generally thought to be true. (Einstein's theory of **relativity** is a famous

HYPOTHESIS = An idea being tested.

THEORY = A principle that explains specific facts.

LAW = A theory that checks out after repeat testing.

example.) If it checks out every time it is tested, then a theory can become a law or rule. The law of gravity is no longer a theory; no one has ever been able to make something fall anywhere but down. The idea that the universe began with a "big bang" remains a theory because it can't be demonstrated under test conditions.

What's the difference between . . .
Arithmetic and Mathematics?

Arithmetic is the addition, subtraction, multiplication, and division of numbers. Mathematics is all that and much more.

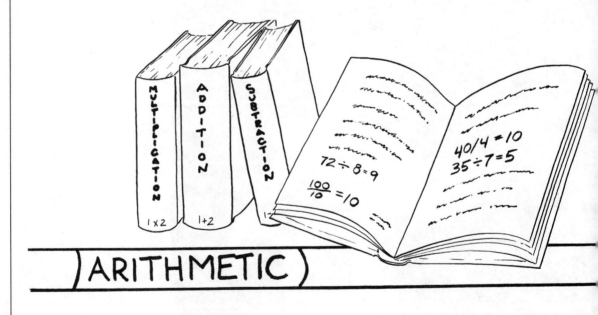

Mathematics is the study of the measurement, properties, and relationships of quantities. It uses numbers and symbols to represent things. In addition to arithmetic, mathematics includes algebra, geometry, trigonometry, calculus, and more.

Did you know?

- In many ways, music is a form of mathematics. In music, notes, rests, and other symbols are used to represent the properties and relationships of sounds.

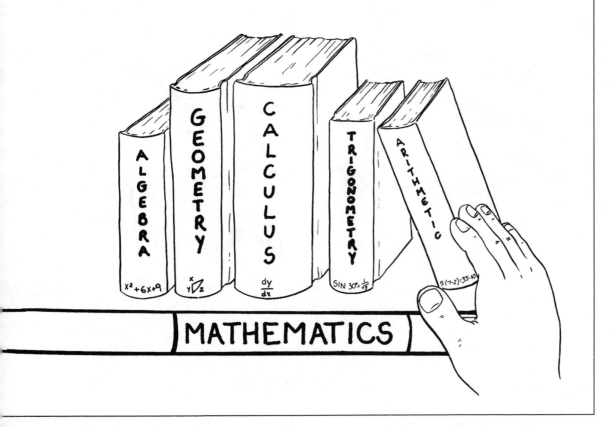

What's the difference between . . .
Cardinal and Ordinal Numbers?

Cardinal numbers are the numbers we use to count or label things, or to answer the question, "How many?" Ordinal numbers are

CARDINAL NUMBERS

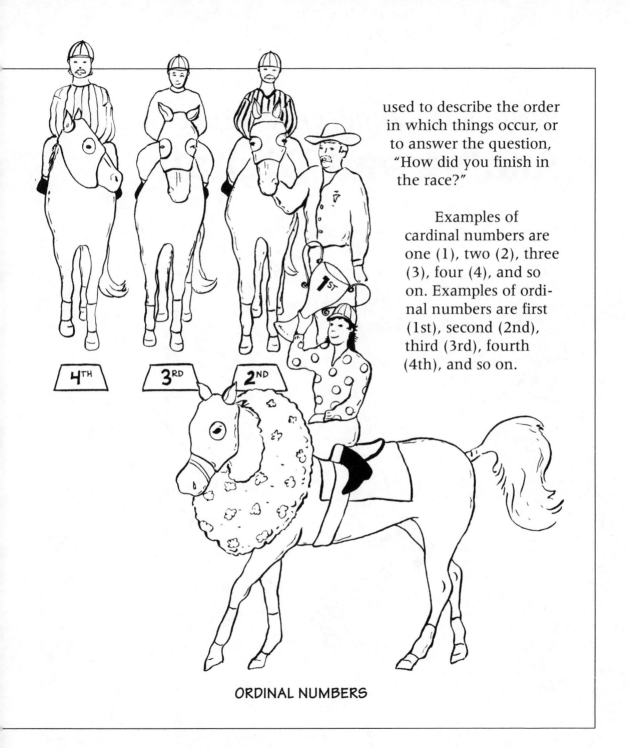

used to describe the order in which things occur, or to answer the question, "How did you finish in the race?"

Examples of cardinal numbers are one (1), two (2), three (3), four (4), and so on. Examples of ordinal numbers are first (1st), second (2nd), third (3rd), fourth (4th), and so on.

ORDINAL NUMBERS

What's the difference between . . .
Analog and Digital?

The best way to explain the difference between analog and digital is with timepieces. A digital watch displays the time by showing numbers, or digits. An analog watch displays the time as relative distances on a dial.

The word "digital" comes from the Latin word for "toe" or "finger." That's how we got our base-10 numbering

ANALOG

system. You can count all ten fingers, and then you have to start the series all over again: 10s, 20s, 30s, and so on. A digital computer is like a machine that counts fingers really fast.

"Analog" comes from a Greek word that means "proportionate." A proportion is a measurable relationship between things. A map is an analog of a real place, because an inch on the map represents a given number of miles or kilometers on the ground.

Digital computers use numbers to do their work, usually just 1 and 0. Analog computers use something else to represent the thing being calculated: **volts** for degrees of temperature, say. So, if 2 volts represent 1 degree of temperature, then 4 degrees would be 8 volts.

DIGITAL

What's the difference between . . .
Fahrenheit and Celsius?

Both Fahrenheit and Celsius are scales for measuring temperature. But they measure it against different numbering systems.

The Fahrenheit scale is the oldest of the temperature-measuring scales. It was invented by Gabriel Daniel Fahrenheit of Germany, who also invented the mercury thermometer, in 1714. In the Fahrenheit scale, water freezes at 32 degrees (32°F) and boils at 212°F. That's a difference of 180 degrees. On most scales, zero is a meaningful starting point. But zero

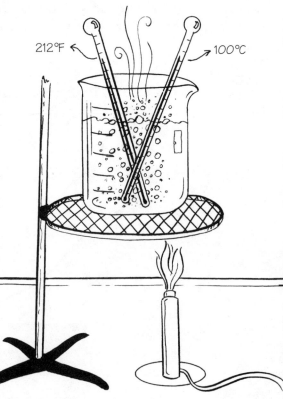

212°F ←   → 100°C

degrees (0°F) has no scientifically useful meaning in the Fahrenheit scale.

Anders Celsius of Sweden had a better idea. In 1742 he invented a scale in which the freezing temperature of water was set at 0°C and the boiling temperature at 100°C. Because of this 100-degree range, the Celsius scale is sometimes called centigrade.

Scientists also use a couple of other scales—Kelvin and Réaumur—for measuring the temperature of things that are very hot or very cold.

Did you know?

- At minus 40 degrees, the Fahrenheit and Celsius scales cross. In other words, –40°F is the same as –40°C. It's the only temperature at which the same numbers have the same meaning.

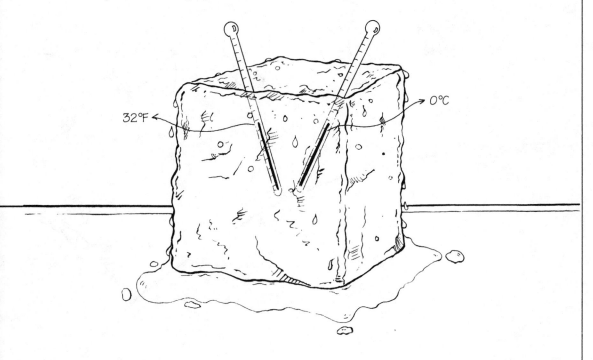

32°F

0°C

What's the difference between . . .
Cycles and Phases?

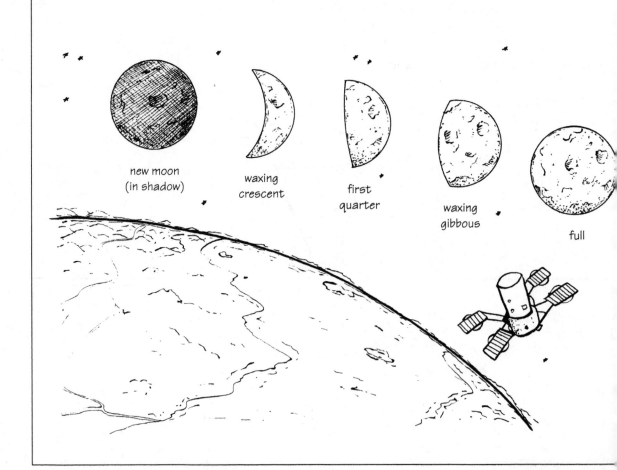

new moon
(in shadow)

waxing
crescent

first
quarter

waxing
gibbous

full

Both cycles and phases are stages in a process, but there the similarity ends. Cycles always go back to the beginning and start over again. Phases are stages in a process which may or may not be repeated.

All cycles have phases, but phases may or may not be part of cycles. For example, we all go through the toddler phase, but just once, thank goodness. The phases of the moon (full, quarter, and new) are parts of the lunar cycle, because they repeat every month.

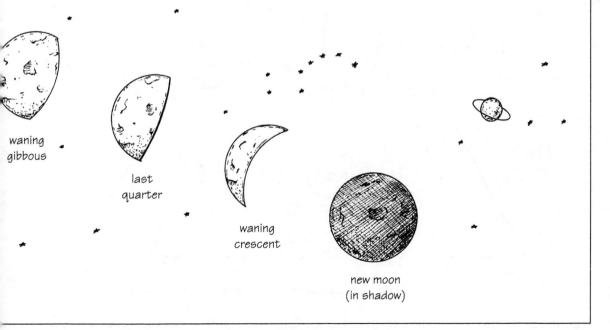

waning
gibbous

last
quarter

waning
crescent

new moon
(in shadow)

What's the difference between . . .
Mass and Weight?

Mass is the amount of matter an object contains. Weight is the gravitational force on a mass.

Mass is measured in terms of how much force is required to move an object, or to speed it up by a certain amount. A body's

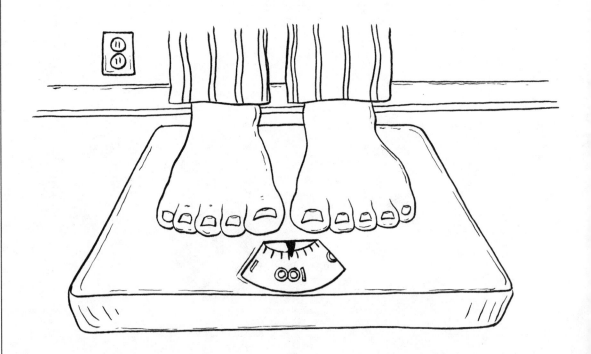

mass remains the same wherever it is, but its weight depends on its distance from the source of gravity and the force of the gravity.

As long as things are measured on the earth's surface, mass and weight are more or less the same (which is why we get them confused). If you could weigh yourself at home on the bathroom scale, and then again on the surface of the moon, you'd see a big difference in weight. For example, if you weighed 100 pounds (45 kg) at home, the moon's weaker gravitational force would only pull you down until the scale hit about 16 pounds (7.2 kg). But your mass would be the same, because you'd still have the same amount of skin, bones, blood, and so on.

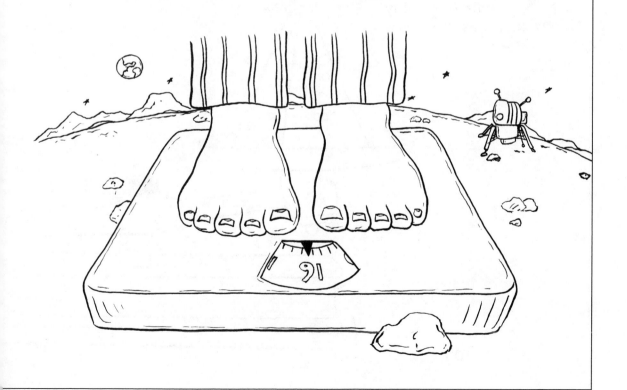

What's the difference between . . .
Tons and Tonnes?

Tons and tonnes are both measures of weight. Tonnes are metric, tons are not.

One tonne equals 1,000 kilograms, or about 2,205 pounds. One ton weighs 2,000 pounds, or roughly 907 kilograms.

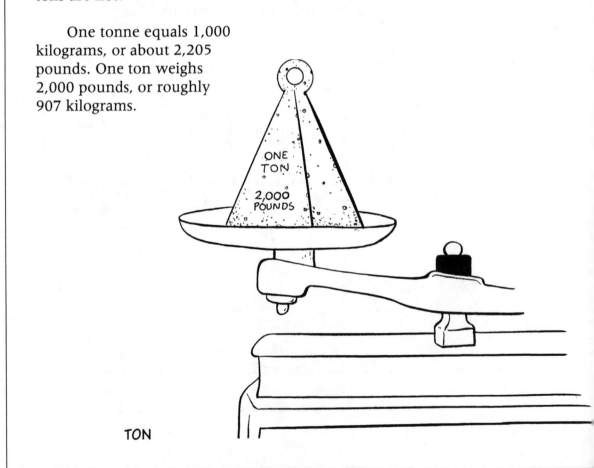

TON

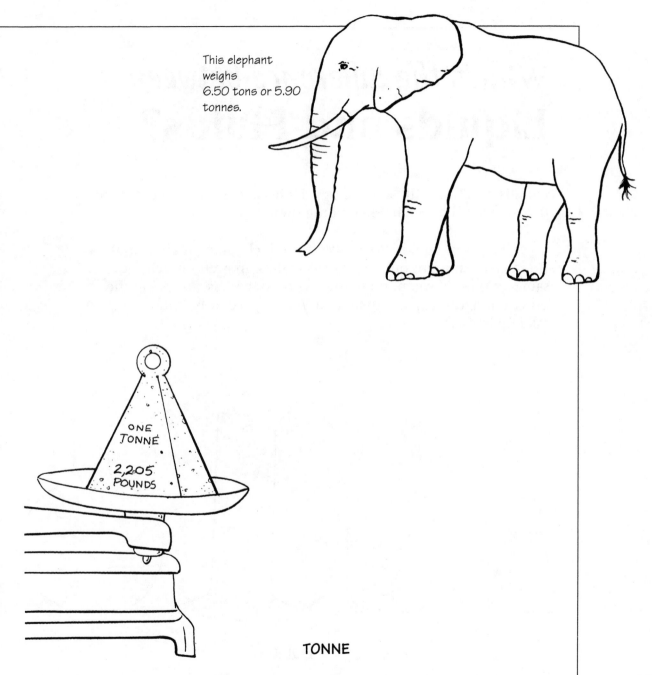

This elephant weighs 6.50 tons or 5.90 tonnes.

ONE TONNE

2,205 POUNDS

TONNE

What's the difference . . .
Liquids and Fluids?

Liquids *are* fluids. But so are gases. Fluids are substances that take the shape of the containers holding them.

Like gases, liquids can move around, changing their shapes. But a given amount of liquid always takes up pretty much the same amount of room, no matter what shape it is. Gases, on the other hand, can expand to take up more space or be compressed to take up less space.

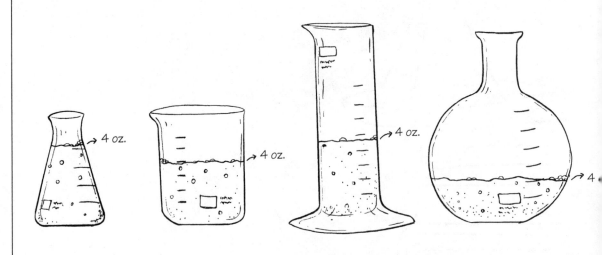

4 oz.

4 oz.

4 oz.

4

LIQUIDS

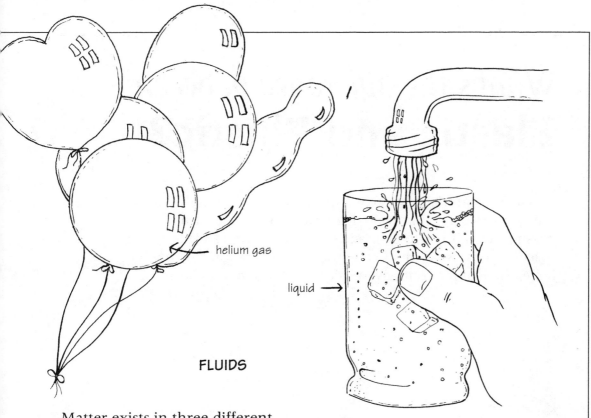

helium gas

liquid →

FLUIDS

Matter exists in three different states: solid, gas, and liquid. Many substances can exist in all three states. Water, for example. As plain, old water, it's a liquid. Frozen as ice, it's a solid. Boiling water turns it into steam, a gas. Water can also be turned into a gas by evaporation. Then it's called water vapor rather than steam.

As you've probably guessed from the example of water, raising or lowering temperatures can cause substances to go from one state to another. So can changes in pressure.

Did you know?

- Snow is a mixture of matters: solids (ice crystals) and a gas (the air that is trapped between the crystals).

- Glass is more like a liquid than a solid. Glass is actually cooled liquid sand. Unlike true solids, glass does not have a definite melting point. The more you heat it, the softer it gets. Like really, really thick syrup or molasses, glass flows. An old pane of glass is always thicker at the bottom than at the top because of gravity.

What's the difference between . . .
Elastic and Plastic?

If, when a material is stretched or pressed into a new shape, it pretty much stays that way, the material is plastic. (But that doesn't mean it has to be made out of what we call "plastic," a specific type of man-made material.) If, when you stop applying force, the material returns to its original shape, it's elastic.

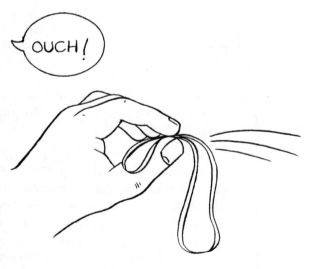

OUCH!

ELASTIC

Rubber is elastic and Silly Putty is plastic. Most materials, even metals, are elastic to some degree or another.

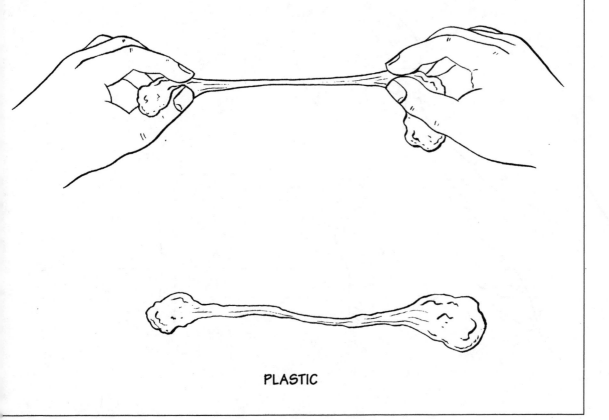

PLASTIC

What's the difference between . . .
Concave and Convex?

Both words are used to describe curved surfaces. The outside surface of a basketball is convex. Its inside surface is concave. If you have trouble remembering which is which, think of a concave surface as caving in.

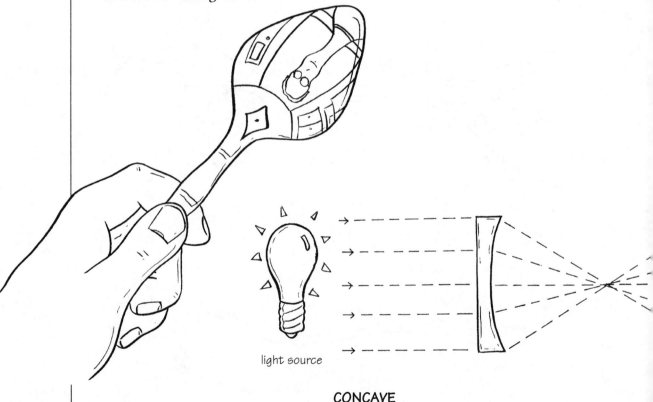

light source

CONCAVE

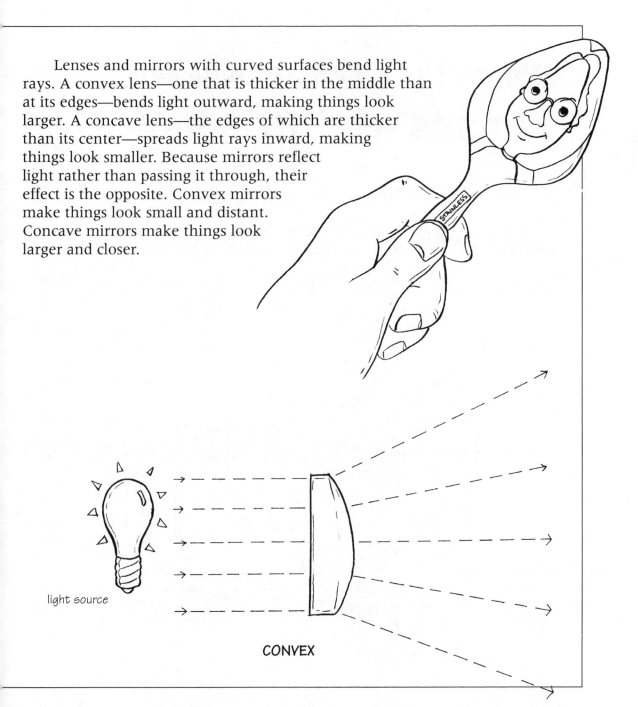

Lenses and mirrors with curved surfaces bend light rays. A convex lens—one that is thicker in the middle than at its edges—bends light outward, making things look larger. A concave lens—the edges of which are thicker than its center—spreads light rays inward, making things look smaller. Because mirrors reflect light rather than passing it through, their effect is the opposite. Convex mirrors make things look small and distant. Concave mirrors make things look larger and closer.

light source

CONVEX

What's the difference between . . .
Lenses and Prisms?

Both refract, or bend, light, but they work differently.

Lenses usually have two curved surfaces (or, one curved and one flat surface) that bend rays of light. Eyeglasses, cameras, mag-

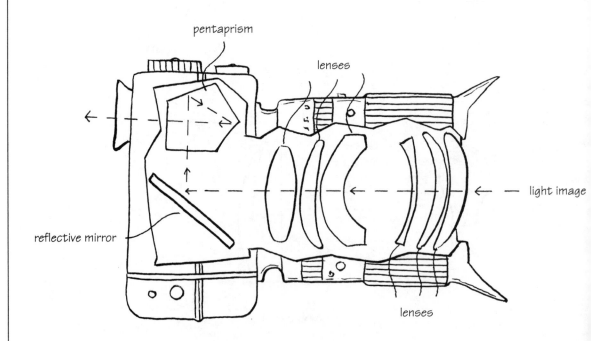

pentaprism

lenses

light image

reflective mirror

lenses

nifying glasses, binoculars, telescopes, microscopes, searchlights, and lighthouses all use lenses to focus light, and some of them can change the size of the image we see.

Prisms are usually three-sided. A prism's sides are angled so that when they bend light they either reflect it in a different direction or separate its colors in a rainbow, which is the color **spectrum**. Gems and cut crystals are prisms that get their glitter from reflected and rainbowed light. Submarine periscopes use prisms as light-bending "mirrors."

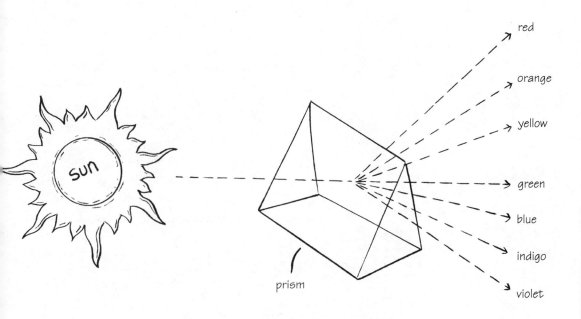

25

What's the difference between . . .
Radiation and Radioactivity?

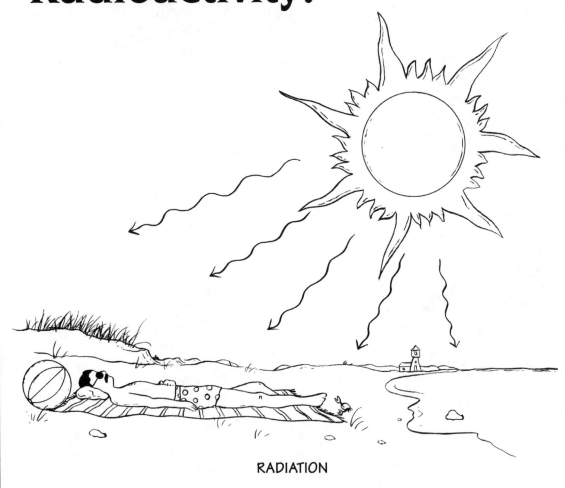

RADIATION

In physics, radiation refers to the act or process by which waves of energy are sent out through space, air, water, or some other medium.

Radioactivity is a special and dangerous kind of radiation, caused by nuclear reactions or natural reactions in radioactive substances, such as uranium.

In everyday use, radiation is simply the act or process of spreading outward. For example, bicycle spokes radiate from the hub or axle to the outer rim of the wheel.

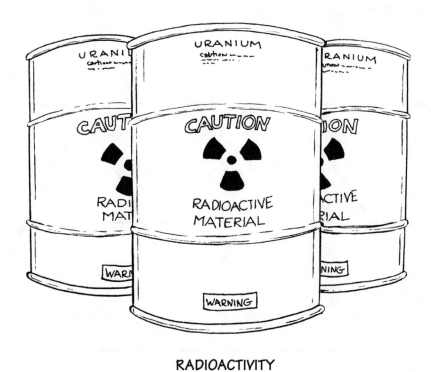

RADIOACTIVITY

What's *the difference between . . .*
Wavelength, Frequency, and Amplitude?

As energy travels along in a wave, its motion creates a waveform of peaks (high points) and troughs (low points). The distance from the top of one wave peak to another is the wavelength. The frequency is the speed of a wave's passage measured in the number of wave-

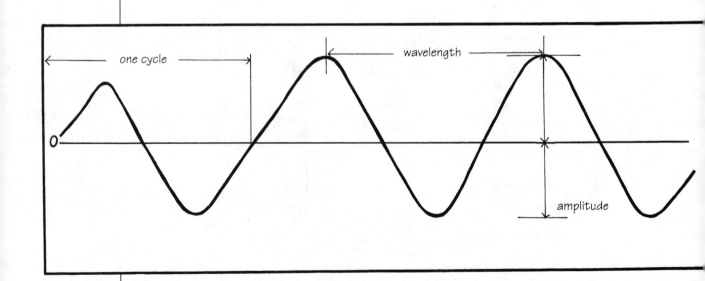

lengths per second past a given point. The distance from the center to the top of a peak or the bottom of a trough is the amplitude.

Differences in wavelength, frequency, and amplitude affect the energy being carried. The shorter the wavelength, the greater the energy. That's why shortwave radio broadcasts can be picked up so far away, compared to regular AM or FM broadcasts.

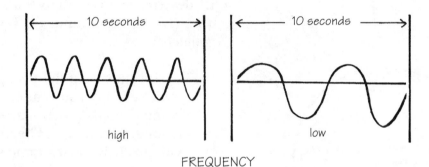

FREQUENCY

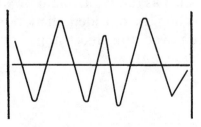

FREQUENCY MODULATION (FM)

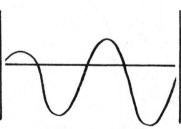

AMPLITUDE MODULATION (AM)

What's the difference between . . .
Incandescent and Fluorescent?

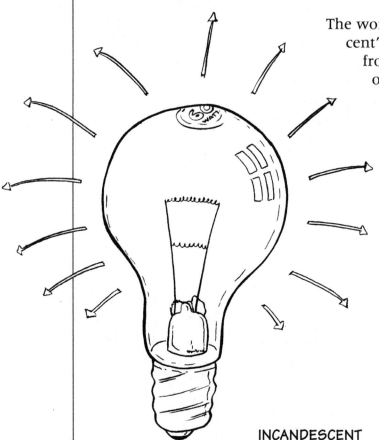

INCANDESCENT

The words "incandescent" and "fluorescent" describe forms of light that come from two different kinds of glowing objects.

Incandescent light is light emitted from a substance that is being heated. When matter is heated, its molecules begin to vibrate. This causes some substances to glow.

Fluorescent light is produced by a material that is absorbing radiation from another source, such as ultraviolet light or x rays. When the outside radiation is removed, the object stops fluorescing (glowing).

The incandescent lightbulb, invented by Thomas A. Edison in 1879, is nothing more than a sealed glass "bottle" enclosing a filament of very thin wire. When the filament is heated by electricity, it glows.

The fluorescent lights we know from home and school are tubes filled with a gas (such as mercury vapor) that can be "excited" by electricity. In its excited state, the gas emits radiation that is absorbed by a special powdery coating inside the tube, which then emits light.

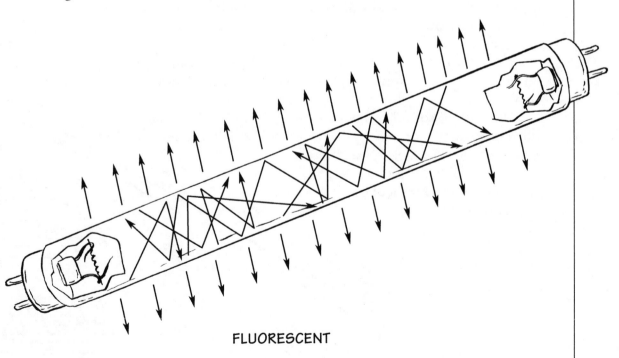

FLUORESCENT

What's the difference between . . .
Sound and Noise?

Sound is what we hear. Noise is sound that's either unorganized or unwanted. Radio static is unorganized sound. Heavy metal rock is music if we want to hear it, but it's noise if we don't.

Sound is a moving waveform. What we actually hear is not sound itself but a sound **sensation**, the response of our ears to sound waves. The sound wave can be a wave of pressure or of moving particles. Some sound waves can be felt, but not heard. When an **audible** sound wave strikes our ears, it causes a response we can hear.

The pressure of a sound wave is called either volume or loudness. "Volume" applies to the intensity of the sound itself and "loudness" to the way we hear the sound. The intensity of sound can be expressed in units called decibels.

A person with good hearing can detect sounds down to between 1 and 5 decibels. Soft leaves stirring in a light

50

40

one
typewriter

30

soft
whisper

20

NOISE

10

human
heartbeat

0

faintest audible sound

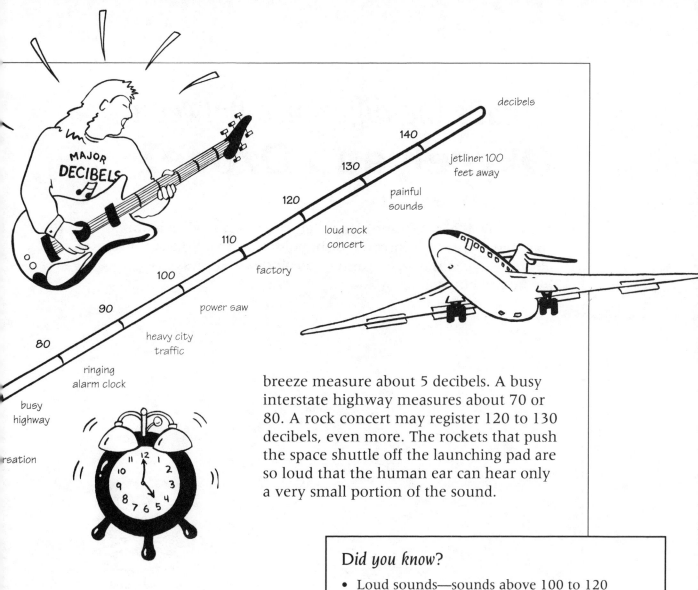

breeze measure about 5 decibels. A busy interstate highway measures about 70 or 80. A rock concert may register 120 to 130 decibels, even more. The rockets that push the space shuttle off the launching pad are so loud that the human ear can hear only a very small portion of the sound.

Did you know?

- Loud sounds—sounds above 100 to 120 decibels—can cause permanent hearing loss. Many rock musicians are partially deaf because they spend so much time around very loud sounds. Loud sound may be music to your ears, but it can be trouble, too.

What's the difference between . . .
Oxygen and Ozone?

Ozone, O3, is a special form of oxygen in which oxygen atoms combine in threes to form a bluish, poisonous gas. What we usually call oxygen is oxygen gas, O2, a colorless, odorless gas formed by the combination of two atoms of oxygen.

ozone layer

smog

oxygen

Oxygen is one of the most important elements on earth. Life on our planet wouldn't be possible without it.

In the upper atmosphere, ozone forms a shield that protects us from getting too much solar radiation. Without this shield, the sun would kill every living thing on earth. Yet, closer to the ground, ozone is a problem. It combines with other chemicals to form smog and other forms of air pollution.

Whatever form it takes, oxygen makes up about a fifth of the earth's atmosphere. Combined with hydrogen, oxygen forms water (H_2O), which covers three-fourths of the earth's surface. Oxygen is also the most abundant element in the earth's crust.

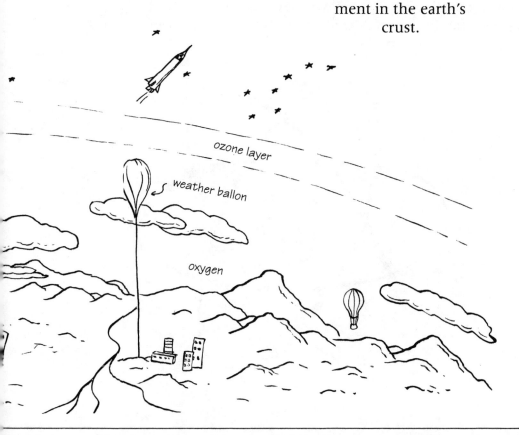

ozone layer

weather ballon

oxygen

What's the difference between . . .
Atoms and Molecules?

Atoms are the smallest part of any substance that can exist and still have the basic chemical properties of the substance. Molecules are the smallest naturally occurring particles of a substance.

Most molecules are formed when two or more atoms become bonded together by a chemical reaction. But some molecules

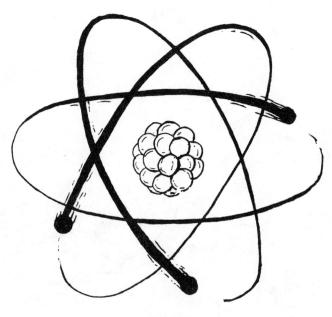

ATOM

contain just a single atom. A substance that contains only one kind of atom is called an **element**. Molecules that contain the atoms of two or more elements are called compounds. It takes a chemical reaction to cause different atoms to form bonds strong enough to hold them together in a molecule.

nitric oxide

nitrogen dioxide

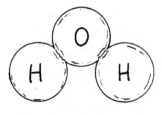

H_2O

ozone

MOLECULES

What's the difference between . . .
Protons, Neutrons, and Electrons?

Protons, neutrons, and electrons are the basic parts of the atom. Protons have a positive electrical charge. Neutrons have no electrical charge and electrons have a negative electrical charge.

Together, protons and neutrons make up the **nucleus**, or center, of the atom. Whirring around

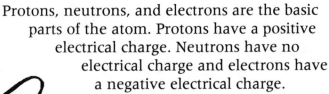

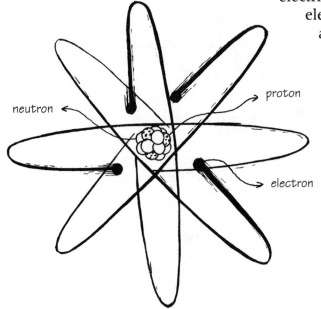

neutron

proton

electron

the nucleus, like the planets in a solar system, are the electrons. But unlike planets, which are solid "balls," electrons have no mass. They are bundles of energy that move almost with the speed of light. Traditionally, atoms are illustrated with their electrons orbiting around their electrons orbiting around their nuclei. But electrons don't actually revolve in circular orbits. Instead, they form spherical "shells" around the nucleus. Some atoms have a single shell of electrons, while others have as many as seven shells.

Every atom has an identical number of protons and electrons. The hydrogen atom has only one of each, and no neutrons. Other atoms may have different numbers of neutrons. The most common form of carbon is called carbon-12 because it has six protons and six neutrons. Radioactive carbon-14 has six protons and eight neutrons.

Did you know?

- The word "atom" is from a Greek word that means "indivisible." Atoms were once thought to be the smallest things in nature. Now we know about subatomic particles, such as protons, neutrons, and electrons. In fact, more than 200 kinds of subatomic particles are known to exist.

What's the difference between . . .
Fission and Fusion?

Fission is a splitting or breaking apart of something. Fusion is the act or process of combining.

Fission and fusion are often referred to as forms of atomic, or nuclear, energy. In nuclear fission, a high-speed neutron smashes into an atom's nucleus, causing it to split apart. When a nucleus splits in two, matter is converted to energy and extra neutrons are emitted. These neutrons smash into and break apart other nuclei

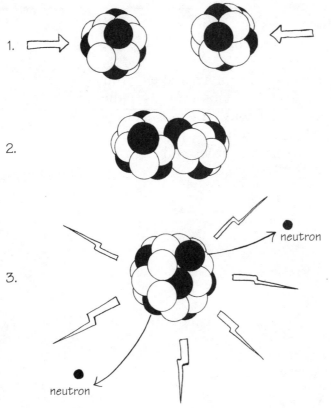

1.

2.

3.

neutron

neutron

FUSION

in what is known as a "chain reaction." Vast amounts of energy are released during this process.

Fusion is a similar process, but it is not caused by bombarding nuclei with neutrons. Instead, two different nuclei are slammed together, creating a new nucleus. The new nucleus then releases energy and extra neutrons, starting a chain reaction.

Did you know?

- The sun and all the other stars in the universe are powered by nuclear fusion. Heat and light are released by this chain reaction.

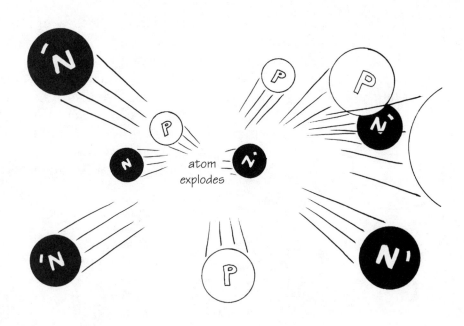

atom explodes

FISSION

What's the difference between . . .
Static Electricity and Current Electricity?

Static electricity doesn't flow. Current electricity does.

Current electricity is the flow of electrons from one place to another. Static electricity simply builds up until it discharges by jumping as a spark from one charged body to another. Current electricity is more useful than static electricity because it can be sent through wires to make it do work where we want it to. Static electricity is often created by friction between two different materials.

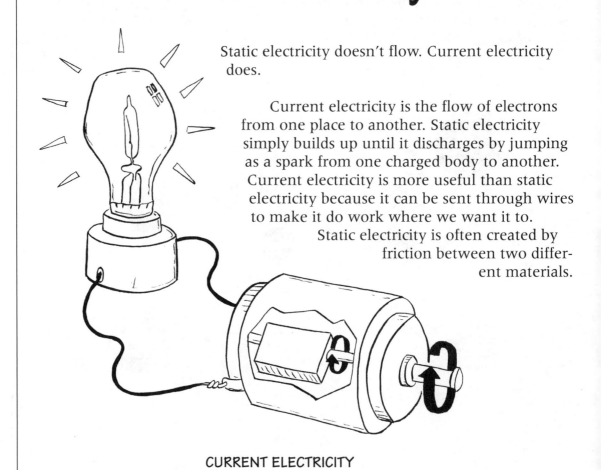

CURRENT ELECTRICITY

Why? Because all matter is made of atoms, which contain an equal number of positively charged protons and negatively charged electrons. When two objects are rubbed together, some of the electrons jump from one material to the other. One of the objects becomes negatively charged, because it has too many electrons, and the other becomes positively charged because it has too few.

When you walk across a rug, then reach for a metal door knob, a spark of static electricity may jump between your fingers and the knob, shocking you. It's just your body getting rid of the extra electrons it picked up from the friction between you and the rug.

STATIC ELECTRICITY

Technology

What's the difference between . . .
Minerals and Metals?

METALLIC

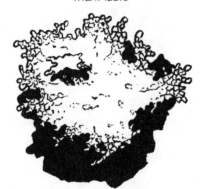

copper

Metals are a special kind of mineral.

    Minerals are the materials that make up rocks. Minerals occur naturally in the earth. They are **inorganic** (which means they are not living things). Minerals include things like marble and salt as well as metals.

NONMETALLIC

rock
groundmass

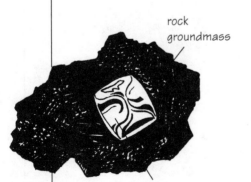

diamond

rock salt

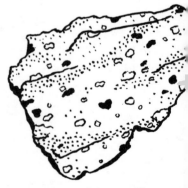

olivine marble

MINERALS

Metals are minerals that have certain properties. They are usually shiny and are good conductors of heat and electricity. Metals can be pressed, hammered, bent, or drawn into various shapes without breaking.

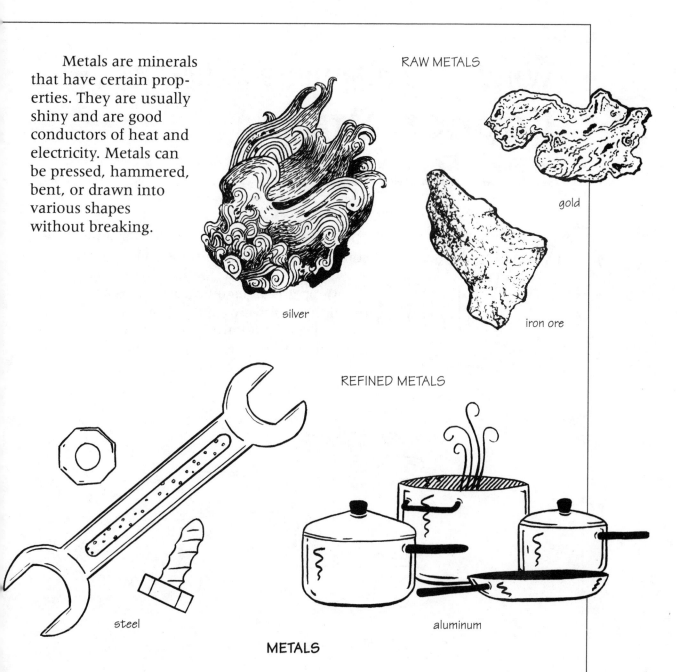

RAW METALS

gold

silver

iron ore

REFINED METALS

steel

aluminum

METALS

What's the difference between . . .
Copper, Brass, and Bronze?

These metals look pretty much alike and all contain at least some of the element copper.

Copper is an element, as well as a **refined** metal that is mostly copper. Brass is a metal **alloy**, a combination of copper and zinc. Bronze is an alloy of copper and tin. Some bronzes also contain one or more other metals, such as zinc, nickel, or lead.

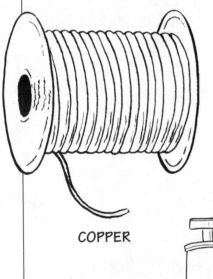

COPPER

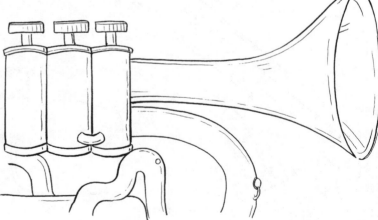

BRASS

Trumpets, trombones, tubas, sousa-phones, French horns, and some other wind instruments are collectively called brass instruments because they are made mostly of brass. Saxophones are also made of brass, but because of their reeds (originally made of bamboo) they are classified as reed instruments or woodwinds. The Wood-winds also include clarinets, oboes, and bassoons.

Did you know?

• Pennies are no longer made of copper. Today's pennies are made of copper-plated zinc. Copper is too expensive to use for pennies. But dimes, quarters, and half dollars *are* made of copper (not silver), which is plated with an alloy of copper and nickel. Speaking of nickel, the five-cent piece of that name is made from an alloy that uses three times as much copper as nickel. Silver dollars aren't made any more at all. At least paper money is still made of paper!

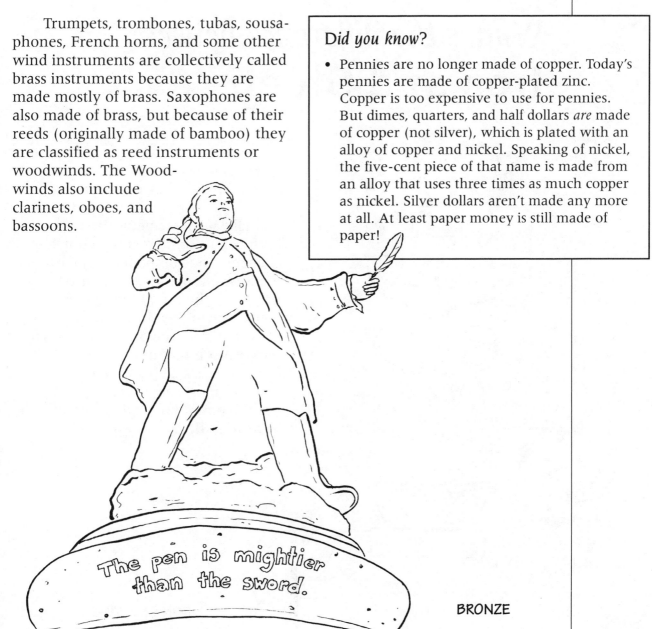

The pen is mightier than the sword.

BRONZE

49

What's the difference between . . .
Iron and Steel?

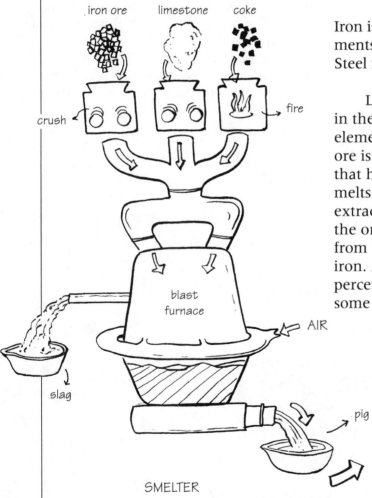

iron ore limestone coke

crush

fire

blast
furnace

AIR

slag

pig iron

SMELTER

IRON SMELTING

Iron is one of the basic chemical elements of which the earth is formed. Steel is an alloy based on iron.

Like most elements, iron is found in the earth combined with other elements and compounds. The iron ore is taken to a smelter, a furnace that heats the ore until the metal melts. The molten iron can then be extracted from the other materials in the ore. Iron that has been smelted from ore is called pig iron, or cast iron. Although pig iron is about 95 percent pure iron, it still contains some impurities, especially carbon.

Once most of the carbon has been removed from pig iron, it becomes wrought iron. Look at older buildings and you will often see railings, balconies, and other decorative features made of wrought iron. The blacksmiths in cowboy movies are working wrought iron by heating it to soften it, then hammering it into shape on an anvil. Although wrought iron is used in manufacturing many products, most of it is turned into steel. Steel is made by further refining the wrought iron to remove carbon and other impurities, and by retaining or adding other elements. Steel is harder, stronger, and more difficult to work than wrought iron.

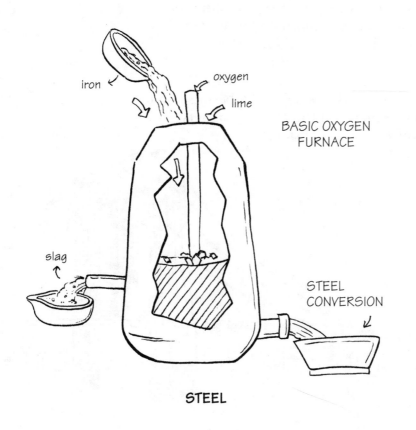

iron

oxygen

lime

BASIC OXYGEN
FURNACE

slag

STEEL
CONVERSION

STEEL

What's the difference between . . .
Steel and Stainless Steel?

Steel is an alloy of iron. Stainless steel is the name given to steel alloys that contain more than 10 percent chromium and other elements such as nickel, silicon, and tungsten.

Stainless steels do not rust or corrode as easily as iron or other steels. And because of all the other elements in the alloys, magnets won't work on stainless steels.

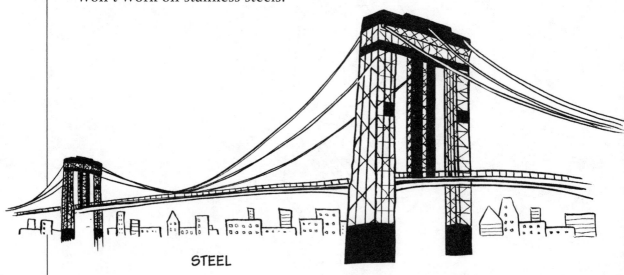

STEEL

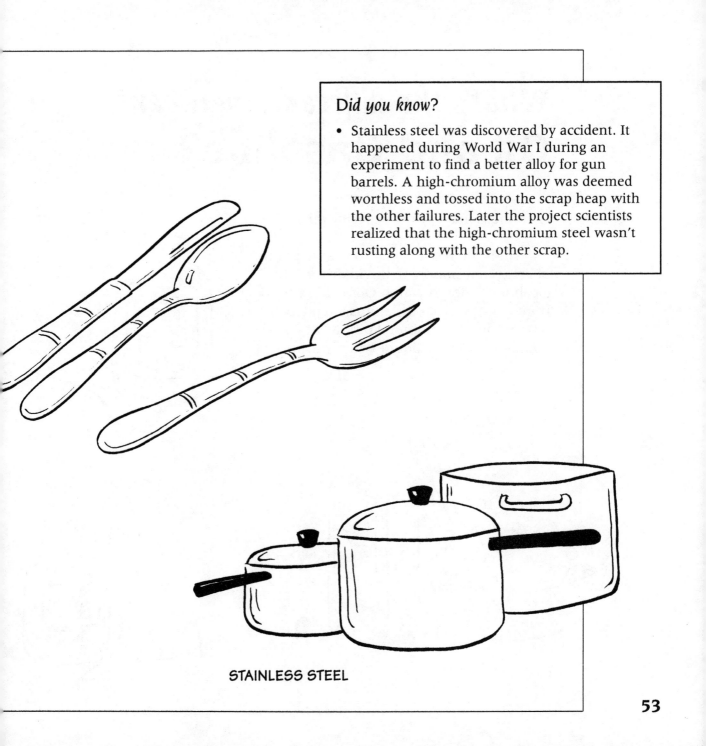

Did you know?

- Stainless steel was discovered by accident. It happened during World War I during an experiment to find a better alloy for gun barrels. A high-chromium alloy was deemed worthless and tossed into the scrap heap with the other failures. Later the project scientists realized that the high-chromium steel wasn't rusting along with the other scrap.

STAINLESS STEEL

What's the difference between . . .
Oil and Gasoline?

Gasoline is made from a specific oil.

Oil is the name given to a large group of greasy substances that will dissolve in alcohol but not in water. Oils can come from plants (olive oil), animals (cod liver oil), or minerals (mineral oil). Most oils are liquids, or become liquid when warmed.

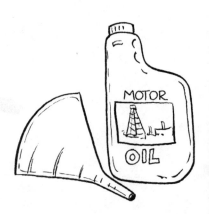

OILS

Gasoline is just one of several products that can be refined from a naturally occurring oil called petroleum. (Petroleum is formed underground by the slow decay of vegetation over thousands of years.) Other products refined from petroleum include kerosene, heating oil, lubricating oils and greases, petroleum jelly, jet fuel, paraffin, paints, dyes, medicines, and a host of useful chemicals called petrochemicals.

> **Did you know?**
>
> • In much of the world, gasoline is called petrol. The American term for gasoline, "gas," is wrong. Gasoline is a liquid, not a gas.

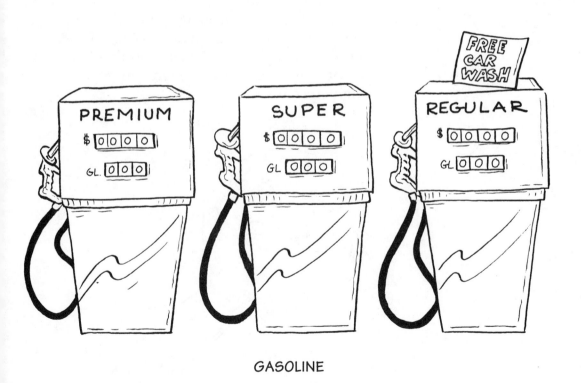

GASOLINE

What's the difference between . . .
Soaps and Detergents?

Soaps are made by combining fatty oils with lye or other strongly **alkaline** chemicals. When the ingredients are mixed together and heated, a chemical reaction occurs between the fatty acids and the alkali.

Detergents are made by combining petro-chemicals that come from oil or coal. Most detergents contain all sorts of chemicals that help remove dirt and grease, whiten whites, and brighten colors.

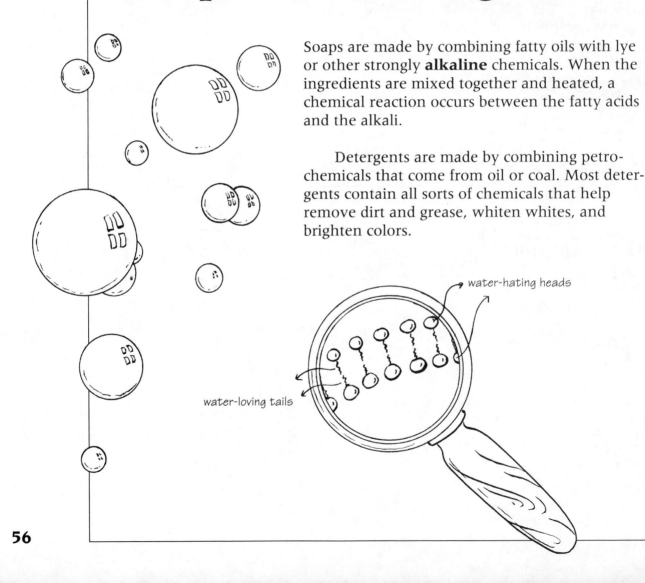

water-hating heads

water-loving tails

Even though they're made differently, soaps and detergents work pretty much alike. Both have molecules with "water-loving" heads and "water-hating" tails. When the molecules encounter a soiled surface, their tails sink into grease deposits, trying to "hide" from the water. Once enough soap or detergent molecules have attached themselves to the grease, the exposed heads are attracted to the molecules of water and lift the grease off the surface. The big disadvantage of soaps, and the reason detergents were developed, is that soaps form a scum when they react with the chemicals in certain kinds of water.

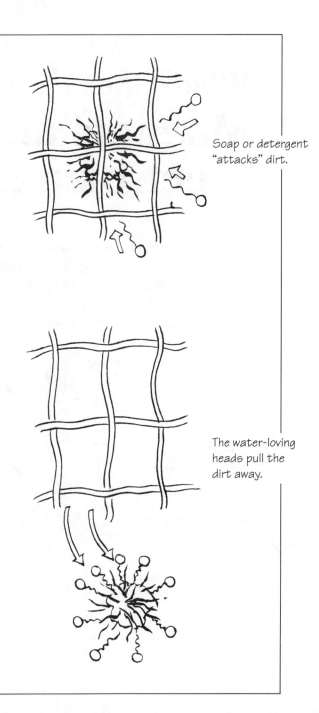

Soap or detergent "attacks" dirt.

The water-loving heads pull the dirt away.

What's the difference between . . .
Magnets and Electromagnets?

Magnets are pieces of iron-based materials that attract iron to themselves by producing an invisible magnetic field. Magnets work because the atoms that make them up are arranged in orderly groups called **domains**. These magnets are sometimes called permanent magnets to distinguish them from electromagnets.

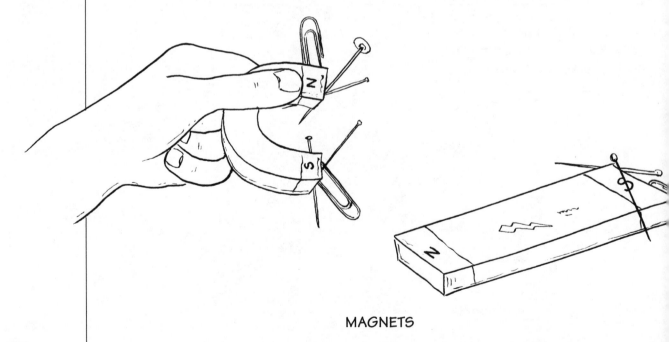

MAGNETS

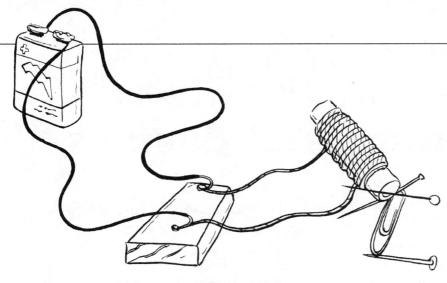

ELECTROMAGNET

Electromagnets are usually made of soft iron which is magnetized when electricity passes through a coil of wire around it. The atoms in a piece of ordinary iron are arranged in no particular order. When the electrical current passes through the iron, it makes the atoms line up in domains, which magnetizes it. When the current is turned off, the piece of iron will no longer act as a magnet. Unlike a permanent magnet, an electromagnet can be made stronger or weaker by changing the strength of an electrical current.

Both permanent magnets and electromagnets have two poles at their opposite ends, north and south. Unlike poles (N–S) attract each other, and like poles (N–N or S–S) repel each other. The magnetic field stretches between the poles.

Did you know?

- Horseshoe magnets are nearly three times stronger than bar magnets of the same size. Because the poles (ends) of the horseshoe magnet are close together, their attractive power is combined.

What's *the difference between* . . .
Motors and Engines?

Motors are devices for converting other forms of energy into **kinetic**, or mechanical, energy. (The words "motor" and "motion" have the same root.) Engines are also energy-converting devices, but their energy output doesn't have to be mechanical. In other words, engines don't have to make anything move to be called engines.

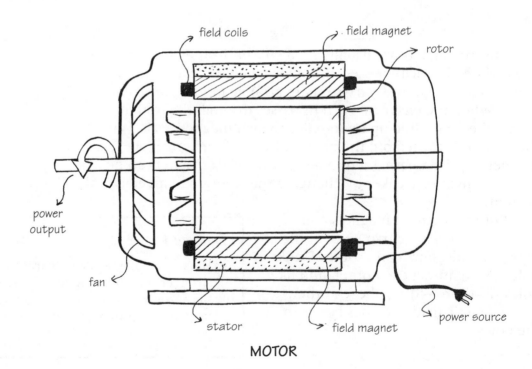

MOTOR

The technical distinction between these words often becomes blurry when we talk about the motors that propel vehicles. If a vehicle is powered by electricity, we nearly always use the word "motor." When we talk about cars, buses, trucks, and motorcycles, we use "engine" more often than "motor," even though these vehicles obviously move. If a car, bus, or truck is diesel powered, we usually say it has a diesel engine. The things that turn airplane propellers may be called both engines and motors. It's the same with space vehicles: You'll hear people talk about rocket motors and rocket engines when they mean the same thing. But we nearly always say jet planes are propelled by jet engines.

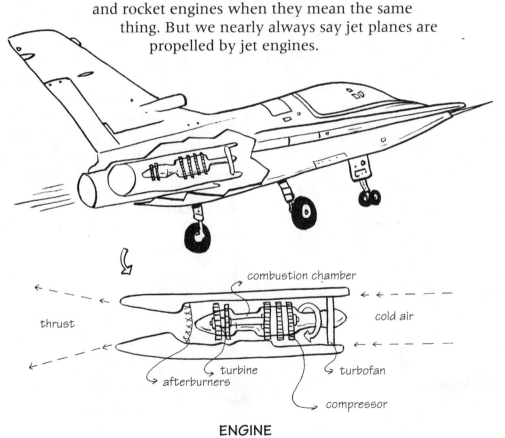

thrust

combustion chamber

cold air

afterburners

turbine

turbofan

compressor

ENGINE

What's the difference between . . .
Cranes and Derricks?

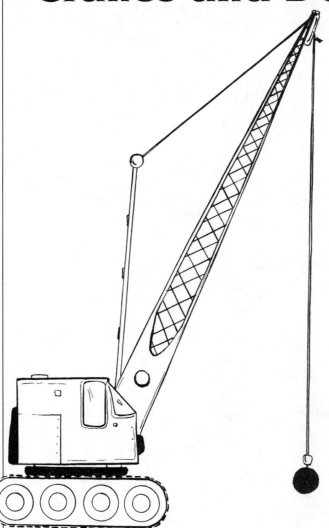

Both are machines that use cables and pulleys for hoisting heavy industrial equipment. Cranes have movable **booms** (or arms) mounted on top of a supporting structure that moves around. The movable booms on derricks are attached to an upright, stationary beam or structure. The tall, usually triangular frameworks over oil wells are called derrick cranes, stiffleg derricks, or Scotch derricks.

CRANE

Did you know?

• Our word "derrick" comes from "derick," meaning "hangman," after a sixteenth-century English hangman named Derick.

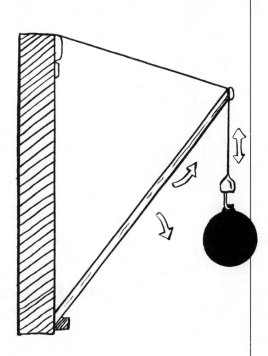

DERRICKS

63

What's the difference between . . .
Cement and Concrete?

Cement is a dry powder made by grinding limestone and clay or by mixing together such compounds as silica, alumina, lime, iron oxide, and magnesia. Cement is mixed with water and hardens when dry.

Concrete is a mixture of water, **aggregate** (the collective name for substances like sand, gravel, or crushed rock), and binding material, which is usually cement.

water, cement, and sand or gravel

CONCRETE

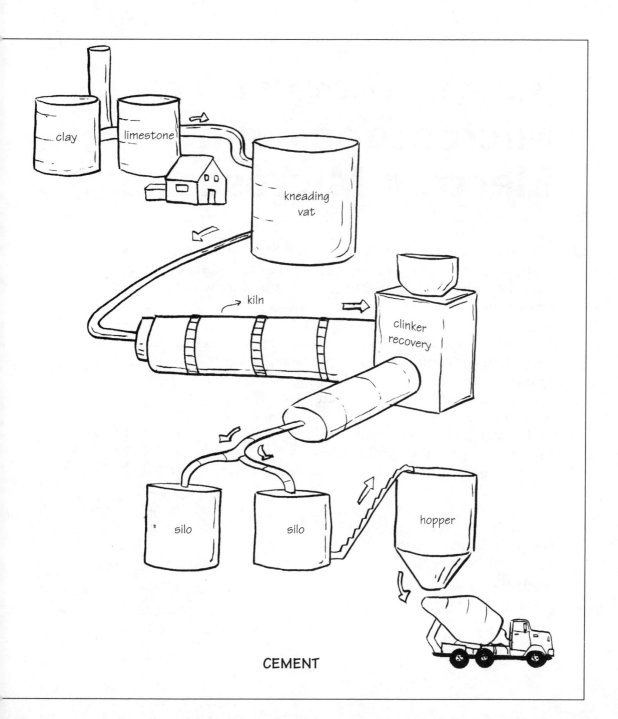

CEMENT

What's *the difference between . . .*
Microscopes and Electron Microscopes?

Microscopes are instruments through which tiny objects can be enlarged many times. Regular microscopes use light and lenses to magnify objects up to 2,000 times. Electron microscopes use electrons rather than light and lenses to magnify.

Electron microscopes can magnify things more than a million times with the help of electromagnetic fields. Electron microscopes don't use light or lenses. Instead, a heated wire filament sends a beam of electrons to the object under examination. Depending on how dense the object is, all, most, some, or none of the electrons pass through. The electrons that get through strike a photographic plate or a television screen to create a shadow picture of the object, magnified many times.

eyepiece lens

objective lenses

object

condenser lens

mirror

MICROSCOPE

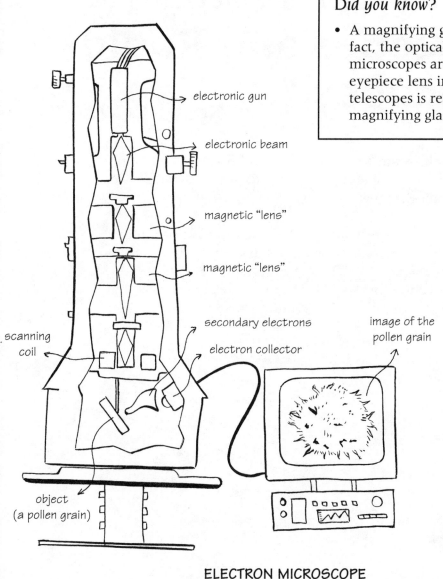

electronic gun

electronic beam

magnetic "lens"

magnetic "lens"

secondary electrons

image of the pollen grain

scanning coil

electron collector

object (a pollen grain)

ELECTRON MICROSCOPE

What's the difference between . . .
Telescopes and Radio Telescopes?

Telescopes use lenses and/or mirrors to bend, focus, and magnify light waves so we can see distant objects. Radio telescopes collect radio waves rather than light waves.

Telescopes that magnify light waves are called optical telescopes. Optical telescopes must be aimed directly at their targets and can only see those objects in space that emit or reflect light.

Radio telescopes allow us to "see" really distant objects that **astronomers** call radio stars. These radio stars emit radio waves

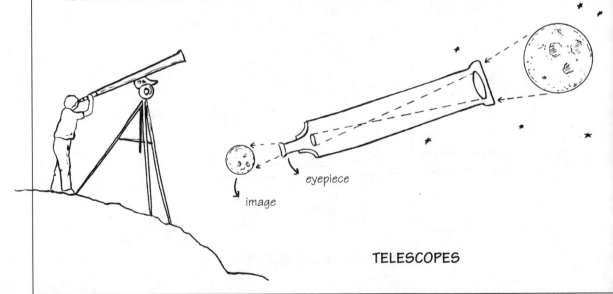

eyepiece

image

TELESCOPES

RADIO TELESCOPE

which are collected by large dishes (similar to the dish antennas used by TV stations). Radio telescopes must be much larger than optical telescopes to gather the same amount of information. Radio telescope dishes do not have to be aimed directly at their targets, because they can collect radio waves striking from any direction. Besides having much greater power and range, radio telescopes can be used on cloudy days when optical telescopes are useless.

Did you know?

- Galileo did not invent the telescope. The telescope was invented by a Dutch eyeglass maker named Hans Lippershey in 1608. He discovered it quite by accident, when he held two lenses together and looked through them at a weather vane on a church. But Galileo *was* the first person to use the telescope to study the stars and planets, in 1609.

- The world's largest telescope is 1,000 feet in diameter. It's the radio telescope at Arecibo, Puerto Rico, located inside a natural crater. The world's largest optical telescope is at the Keck Observatory on Mauna Kea in Hawaii. Its lens is about 33 feet, 4 inches across.

What's the difference between . . .
Film and Videotape?

Film is treated with a light-sensitive **emulsion** (a mixture of liquids that dissolve). When the treated film is exposed to light, through the camera's lens, an image is "burned" into the emulsion. Exposed film must be developed before it can be printed or projected for viewing.

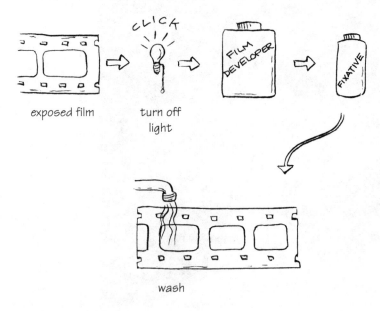

exposed film   turn off light

wash

FILM

Videotape is coated with a fine film of magnetic particles. The videocamera converts the light and sound waves to electromagnetic waves, which rearrange the particles on the tape in ways that videotape players can translate back into waves of light and sound. As soon as the tape has been recorded on, it's ready to be played back. This is similar to the way audiotapes are recorded and played. Tape can be erased and reused many times.

Did you know?

- Until videotapes were invented back in the 1950s, the instant replay now used in broadcast sporting events wasn't possible. Before videotapes, television shows were either shown live, or the shows were recorded on film for later broadcast.

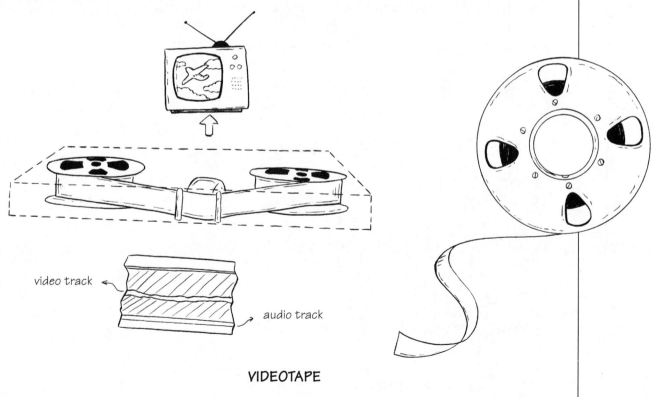

video track

audio track

VIDEOTAPE

What's *the difference between . . .*
Batteries and Dry Cells?

There is no difference in everyday use. But technically, a battery is a series of cells that store chemical energy and convert it to electrical energy. A dry cell is just one electrical cell.

A typical electrical cell has three parts: negative and positive terminals and an **electrolyte**. The electrolyte is a chemical, or mixture of chemicals, that conducts electricity. Chemical reactions in the cell cause electrons to flow out of the negative terminal,

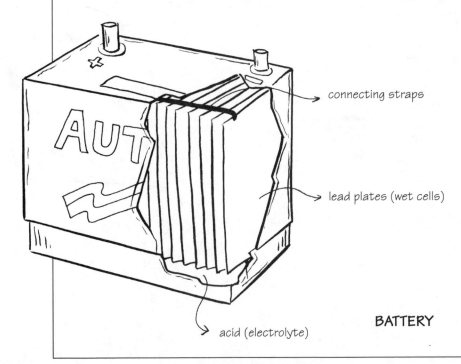

connecting straps

lead plates (wet cells)

acid (electrolyte)

BATTERY

through the bulb or other object being powered, and back through the positive terminal.

The batteries we use to power our portable radios, cassette players, flashlights, toys, wristwatches, and other gadgets are called "dry" cells because the electrolyte is not in liquid form. In most small dry cells, it's a paste.

Besides dry cells, there are also wet cells. In wet cells, the electrolyte is liquid. An automobile battery is a series of wet cells that use lead and acid.

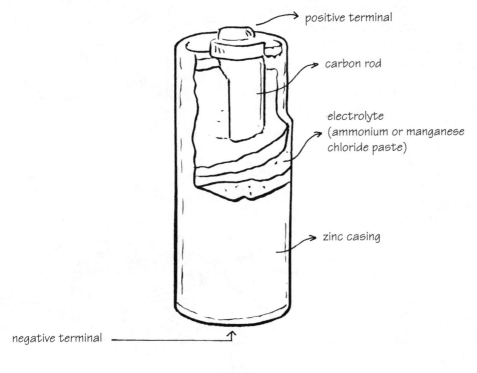

DRY CELL

What's the difference between . . .
Transformers and Transistors?

Transformers are devices used to trans-fer electric energy from one circuit to another. Transistors are small, solid electronic devices used to amplify (strengthen) and control the flow of electrical current in electrical circuits.

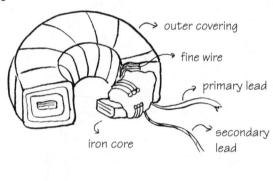

outer covering

fine wire

primary lead

secondary lead

iron core

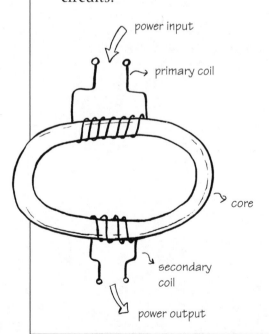

power input

primary coil

core

secondary coil

power output

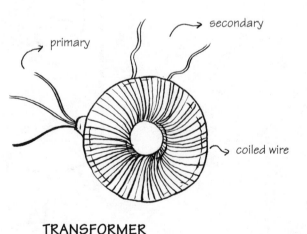

primary

secondary

coiled wire

TRANSFORMER

Transformers can change voltage as well. A simple transformer has two coils of wire wrapped onto the same, doughnut-shaped core of soft magnetic metal. Current is received by the first (primary) coil and passed through the core to the secondary coil. If the secondary coil contains fewer turns (coils) of wire than the primary coil, the voltage will be "stepped down" (decreased). If the secondary coil has more turns, the voltage will be "stepped up" (increased).

Transistors are much smaller than transformers. Transistors are used in radios, televisions, and stereo equipment to make signals more powerful.

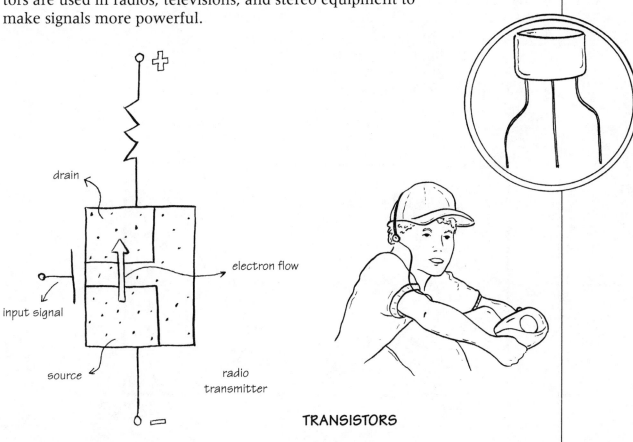

drain

input signal

source

electron flow

radio transmitter

TRANSISTORS

What's the difference between . . .
Radar and Sonar?

As soon as you know where the words came from, you will get a clue to the difference. Radar stands for *ra*dio *det*ection *a*nd *r*anging. Sonar stands for *so*und *na*vigation and *r*anging. ("Radar" and "sonar" are **acronyms**.)

Except that radar uses radio waves and sonar uses sound waves, they work pretty much the same. Waves are transmitted and echoed back when they bounce off an object. By measuring the time it

RADAR

takes the waves to go out and return, it's easy to tell how far away the object is. By measuring which parts of the wave were returned, an object's position, size, and shape can be determined.

Radar was first used to detect enemy airplanes, but now its principal uses are in navigation and air traffic control. Sonar is used to tell ships how deep the water is, to help fishermen find fish, and to help locate reefs, shipwrecks, and other objects on the bottom of the ocean or other body of water. Sonar is also called echo sounding or echolocation.

The sound frequencies used in sonar are usually above the range of human hearing. Such sound is called ultrasound. Ultrasound scanners are also used in medicine to help doctors diagnose diseases in muscles, bones, and other tissues.

Did you know?

- Bats use something very much like sonar to find prey and avoid flying into things after dark. That's why their ears are so big: so they can hear the echoes of the high-pitched squeaks they send out.

- Radar uses microwaves that are similar to the ones used in a microwave oven. One of the first microwave ovens on the market was called the Radarange.

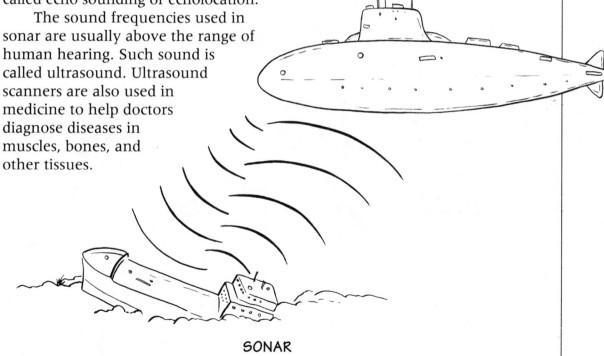

SONAR

77

What's the difference between . . .
Bits and Bytes?

The word "bit" is computer shorthand for *binary* dig*it*, a number in the binary system of numbers. The binary system has just two numbers, 1 and 0. To a computer, 1 means "on" or "yes," and 0 means "off" or "no." That's why computers can work so fast, because they only deal in ons and offs, yeses and nos.

To do any useful work (such as word processing or calculating num-

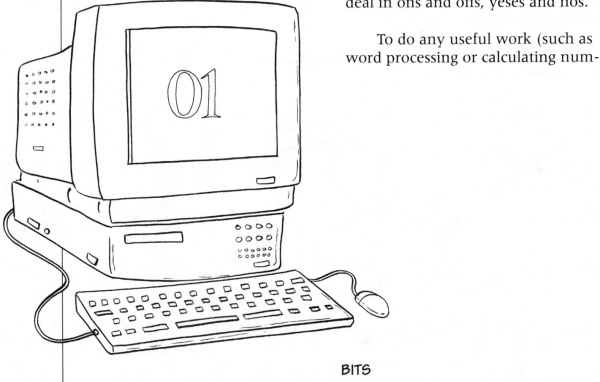

BITS

bers), computers use groups of bits that are assembled to have more meaning than "yes" or "no." These meaningful groups of bits are called bytes. (No one knows for sure, but most think the word "byte" comes from the notion of taking a "bite" of information that isn't too big for a computer to swallow or digest.) Each byte may represent a number, a letter, a punctuation mark, or some other meaningful symbol ($, √, ÷, ♥, and so on).

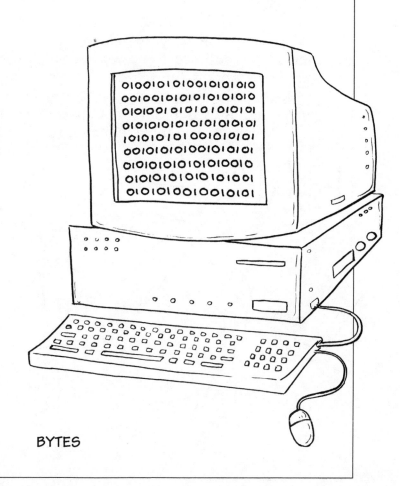

BYTES

What's the difference between . . .
RAM and ROM?

RAM stands for *random-access* memory. ROM stands for *read-only* memory.

Computer memory isn't like human memory. It's better to think of it as desk space or a workbench. It's where all the computer's work is done.

RAM is the main memory (the principal working area) of a computer. It is used to run programs and to juggle things or store them temporarily while the processing or computing is going on. Things that are stored in RAM can be erased, as if they were written on a blackboard.

RAM

ROM is built into the computer on separate memory chips. Computer users cannot write anything in ROM, so anything stored there is more or less permanent. The systems programs that enable the computer to work are permanently stored in ROM. Application programs, like word processors, can also be stored in ROM but are usually stored on disk, which has more room.

RAM and ROM are usually expressed in kilobytes (1,000 bytes) or megabytes (one million bytes). So is disk, or storage, space. Supercomputers and some of the new hard-disk drives for smaller computers measure their capacities in gigabytes, which are billions of bytes. (By the way, "gigabytes" may be pronounced so the first syllable sounds like either "jig" or "gig.")

ROM

What's the difference between . . .
CDs and CD-ROM Disks?

CDs (compact discs) store music and speech and are usually played on stereo systems. CD-ROM (compact disc, read-only memory) disks store all sorts of information (including sound and pictures) that can be used by computers.

CD

CDs and CD-ROMs are made and work in much the same way. A digital code is recorded on a compact disc as a series of tiny pits. In playing back a CD, a laser beam is reflected in different directions by the pits and the flat areas of the shiny disc. The reflected light is turned into electrical signals.

This is Tyrannosaurus rex, one of the predatory dinosaurs.

CD-ROM

Glossary

These brief and simple definitions are meant to help you read and understand this book. They are not complete definitions of the words and terms listed. Please use a dictionary or encyclopedia to find out more about these things.

acronym A word formed from a few letters (often the first or last ones) of all or some of the words of a term. Examples are *radar* (from *radio detection and ranging*) and *sonar* (from *sound navigation and ranging*).

aggregate Collective name for sand, stone, or other mineral materials used in making concrete.

alkali/alkaline *Alkali* is the noun; *alkaline*, the adjective. All chemicals are said to be acid, neutral, or basic. *Alkaline* and *basic* are virtually synonymous, and a strongly basic substance is an alkali.

alloy A substance consisting of two or more metals, or a metal and a nonmetal, usually made by melting them together.

astronomer A scientist who studies planets, stars, comets, or other heavenly bodies and their size, motion, and composition.

audible Heard or capable of being heard; within the range of normal hearing.

boom A long stick or arm sticking out from the mast of a derrick, used to support or guide something that is being lifted or lowered.

domain An orderly group.

electrolyte A substance (often a liquid) in which an electrical current is supported by the movement of ions that are not metallic. (An ion is an atom or group of atoms that has become electrically charged by gaining or losing electrons.) Electrolytes are used to conduct electrical currents when wires and other metallic conductors won't do.

element A substance that is made up of only one kind of atom. An element cannot be split into simpler substances by chemical reaction.

emulsion A mixture of liquids that do not dissolve in each other. In an emulsion, droplets of one or more of the liquids are scattered throughout the other liquid. Salad dressings are emulsions, because oil and water won't dissolve in each other; they must be shaken to remix them before each use.

engineering The development and use of nature's resources and power in ways that are useful to people and society.

inorganic Does not contain carbon; not a living thing.

kinetic   Of or relating to the motion of bodies or objects and the forces or energies associated with those movements.

nucleus   The central part of the atom, made up of protons and neutrons (except in the case of hydrogen, whose nucleus contains only one proton). The atom's electrons "orbit" in shells around the nucleus.

refine   To remove impurities from something. Industrially, mineral ores and crude oil are refined in processing.

relativity   In physics, a theory that considers mass and energy to be equal; that states that a moving object will experience changes in mass, size, and time that are only noticeable at speeds approaching the speed of light; and that deals with related gravitational phenomena.

sensation   A mental process or awareness due to the stimulation of a sense organ, such as the nose or ears.

spectrum   A continuous range or series of objects or phenomena. In physics, the electromagnetic spectrum is the entire range of waves with electrical and magnetic properties, including all visible light and colors, ultraviolet and infrared radiation, radio waves, microwaves, x rays, gamma rays, and cosmic rays.

volt/voltage   *Voltage* is electrical potential difference, the difference in electrical charge between two points. Potential difference is measured in *volts*.

work   The energy used when force is applied over a given distance.

Index

acronyms, 76
aggregate, 64
air pollution, 35
alkali, alkaline, 148
alloy, 52–53, 54, 56–57
  brass, 48
  bronze, 48
  in coins, 49
  steel, stainless steel, 47, 54–55, 56–57
AM/FM broadcasts, 29
Arecibo, Puerto Rico, 69
astronomers, 68
atomic energy, *see* nuclear energy
audible, 32

bats, and sonar, 77
"big bang" theory, 3
boom, 62
brass instruments (musical), 49

carbon, 39, 54–55
cast (pig) iron, 54–55
chain reaction, 41
chemical reaction, 36–37, 50–51, 72–73
compounds, 37
computers, 9, 78–79, 80–81
corrosion, 56

deafness, 33
decibels, 32–33
disk vs. disk, 83
domains, 58–59

echo sounding (echolocation), 77
Edison, Thomas A., viii, 31
Einstein, Albert, 2–3
electricity, vii–viii, 42–43, 47, 59, 60–61, 72–73, 74–75
electrolyte, 72–73
element, 34, 37
emulsion, 70
energy, 27, 28–29, 31, 39, 40–41, 60–61, 72–73, 74–75
engineering, vii

Galileo, 69
gases, 18–19, 31, 34, 37, 49
glass, 19
gravity, 3, 14–15

hearing, 32–33
Hero of Alexandria, viii
hydrogen, 35, 37

ice, 10–11, 19, 43
inorganic, 46
instant replay, 71

jet engine, viii, 61

Keck Observatory, 69
Kelvin scale, 11
kinetic energy, 60–61

laundry detergents, and fluorescent chemicals, 31

light, 22–23, 24–25, 27, 30–31, 41, 66–67, 68,
    70–71
lightbulb, invention of, viii, 31
lightning, 43
Lippershey, Hans, 69
loudness, 32

magnets, and stainless steel, 52
magnifying glass, 67
matter, states of, 18–19
Mauna Kea, Hawaii, 69
microwaves, 77
mirrors, 22–23, 24, 66
moon, 12–13, 15
    gravity on, 15
    phases of, 12-13
music, 5, 32–33, 82–83
    as mathematics, 5
    loud, 32–33
    rock, 32–33
    storage on CD, 82

nuclear energy, 40–41
nuclear reactions, 27
nucleus, nuclei, 38–39, 40–41

periscopes, 25
petrochemicals, 50, 55
petrol, 49
petroleum, 55
pig (cast) iron, 50–51
poles, 59

radio broadcasts, 29
radio stars, 68
Réaumur scale, 11
reed instruments, *see* woodwinds
refining, 49, 52, 54–55
relativity, theory of, 2–3
rubber, 20–21
rust, 56–57

science vs. technology, vii–viii
sensation, 32, 85
Silly Putty, 21
smog, 34–35
snow, 19
solar radiation, 26–27, 35
spectrum, 25
steam turbine, viii

technology vs. science, vii–viii
Tesla, Nikolai, viii

ultrasound, 77
uranium, 27

volts, voltage, 9, 85
volume, 32

water, 10–11, 19, 35, 50–51, 64
waves, 27, 28–29, 32–33, 68–69, 71, 76–77
woodwinds, 49
work, viii
wrought iron, 51